ECOSOCIALIST REVOLUTION:

A MANIFESTO

First edition 2024

ISBN
978-0-902869-52-3

Printed on Recycled Paper

Printed by Anti*Capitalist Resistance
Anticapitalistresistance.org

FOREWORD

In an age of increasing crisis and uncertainty, things clearly cannot carry on the way they are. Something has to give.

People say the system is broken, but what if the system is functioning precisely as it is supposed to? In a world dominated by profit at all cost we can see how the overlapping problems of the modern age – the environmental crisis, growing social inequality, pandemics, the rise of the far right – are all rooted in capitalism.

We are struggling in a global economy that exploits both people and planet. Infinite growth on a finite planet is an irrational economic system and clearly impossible to sustain.

Those in power push for a so called green capitalism which maintains unsustainable consumption levels whilst plundering the global south for raw materials. Politicians talk climate targets but nothing changes.

As a result, the scale of the problem seems insurmountable, leading to feelings of powerlessness.

But this is not the only way to live. Alternatives are not only needed, they are possible and can be achieved. We just need to be confident enough to fight for them. Our alternative to the destruction of capital is an economy that meets human needs based on the collective democratic power of producers and consumers. Such a society will be in a sustainable relationship to other life forms and the environment itself eliminating waste and production for profit. We call this society ecosocialism.

This ecosocialist manifesto was adopted at the Anti*Capitalist

Resistance Conference (ACR) in June 2024. It is not a comprehensive policy document covering every issue but it shows our general approach to fighting against the destructive power of capitalism and our vision of what must replace it.

Ecosocialism has been growing as an idea since the early 2000s with global gatherings in Belem (2009) and Lima (2014). ACR helped organise an ecosocialist conference in London in 2023 attended by over 150 people. We want to help strengthen and build this network, to build a real mass movement around struggle against capitalism in the interests of ending ecocide in the name of profit.

If you agree with this manifesto then get in touch and discuss joining. Radical ideas are just words on a page until we can build a mass movement around them with people willing to fight for a better world, a sustainable future based on radical abundance, genuine democracy, less work and more time to explore and enjoy being human.

ECOSOCIALIST REVOLUTION
A MANIFESTO

"Despite all our accomplishments, we owe our existence to a six-inch layer of topsoil and the fact that it rains."

Paul Harvey

"Environmentalism without class struggle is just gardening."

Chico Mendes

Capitalism is a system of constant capital accumulation for mass commodity production where producers and consumers alike have little or no democratic say over the economy. Capital has an inherent tendency to enclose and commodify, transforming everything into a source of private profit. This means it is in irreparable contradiction with nature.

It's impact on people and the planet has been remarkable but also terrible. Climate scientists have identified nine planetary boundaries our eco-system must operate within to be sustainable. As of 2023 six of the nine boundaries have been breached: climate change; biogeochemical flows (e.g., excessive phosphorus and nitrogen pollution from fertiliser use); biosphere integrity (e.g., extinction rate and loss of insect pollination); system change (e.g., deforestation); novel entities (e.g., pollution from plastics, heavy metals, and what are commonly referred to as "forever chemicals"); and freshwater change (e.g., extreme changes in rainfall).

The internationally agreed target of keeping long term average global temperature increases below 1.5C has been already effectively missed. The fight now is to keep the average temperature increase below 2C. It is clear that none of those in power have any real interest in achieving this, delaying everything until 2050, despite the fact that climate scientists warn that there is an acceleration of global warming.

It is clear that the drive for profit is destructive to us as humans, reducing us to units of production in the interest of our economic masters. We have to work for them otherwise they won't pay us, and we cannot live. Those that help the circulation of their profits are rewarded handsomely; those that do not, such as those that provide care work, clean our streets or are economically inactive are paid the bare minimum. We have a world where essential work is considered 'unproductive' but whatever makes money for the capitalists, no matter how degrading or worthless it is in reality, is exalted as 'productive'. Any shred of shared humanity is mutilated and torn apart in the interests of capital, of nation state, of this thing called 'the economy'.

The bosses work us until old age; they sell us unhealthy foods, causing a global obesity epidemic, and make us build cities to serve capital not people. They even poison us – every human on the planet has permanent chemicals (PFAS) from the use of Teflon. Millions of us have plastic microbeads in our system. Cancer rates are predicted to increase by 55% by 2040, whilst healthcare is mercilessly cut back or privatised.

Capital divides us and exploits us. Capital is racial and gendered, it creates certain jobs in different parts of the world and none in others, it depends on unpaid or underpaid labour for social care and families. It remains a system of mass slavery – there are more slaves on the planet today than during the period of chattel slavery in pre-1865 USA. From the outset, capitalism has defined social worth either the procurement of wealth or the ability to sell one's labour. Through the inability to conform to what is 'normal' for capitalism certain groups are subjected to unequal and differential treatment, resulting in oppressive practices and discrimination.

Why does capitalism do this? This is not an unfortunate byproduct of greed or the result merely of so-called 'excess'. Market competition forces capital to accumulate, but the anarchy of this system leads to *overaccumulation.* Capital is driven to expand to defend its market share, to ensure its legal responsibility to shareholders by making profit. The processes driving the overaccumulation of capital destabilises the natural cycles of the Earth, producing an overaccumulation of carbon, nitrogen or phosphorus, whilst greenhouse gases lead to an *under accumulation* of glacial ice or soil fertility.

Capitalism cannot solve these problems because it can only survive as a system by turning pollution into an 'externality' – a cost to someone other than the polluter. Plastic companies make profit and then the health sector has to deal with the micro plastics in our bodies, or a charity has to clean up plastic waste in the ocean. If oil companies had to factor in the social and environmental consequences of their product then they would not only be unprofitable, but owe a huge historic debt to our planet. This is also true of the mining companies flooding communities with toxic sludge, and soft drink manufacturers depleting water tables. All of these examples are seen as externalities for capital, but are real problems for the rest of us.

Everything is growth. Politicians, economists and journalists obsess about whether GDP is up or down. GDP — the rough market value of all the goods and services produced in a region — is the most crude and reactionary way to measure anything, it doesn't account for human happiness, the quality of work, or sustainable relations to the biosphere. Leaving the Amazon rainforest untouched contributes nothing to GDP, whereas cutting it down and burning it for farmland hugely boosts GDP.

In our present economy we are trapped on the 'treadmill of production', productivity for its own sake. Capitalism is heralded as an efficient system but it is only really efficient at the exploitation of nature and labour for mass production of exchange values – regardless of planetary limits or the impact on people. The development of the productive forces cannot now happen without widespread environmental and social damage. China has industrialised under capitalism, but at huge cost to the global environment. New technologies like electric cars create more extractivist mining. Productivism is destructivism.

This is the basis of what has been called the 'metabolic rift'. This is the idea that humans exist as part of the ecosystem alongside all other life on the planet and the biosphere, though we are unique because we are a thinking and conscious part of it. We have a complex society, the power of language and abstract thought and use tools to transform our environment to our benefit. But under our class-based society we are compelled to do environmentally damaging and destructive work in the interest of profit. Capital has organised our society in such a way that there is a rift (rapidly becoming a gulf) between us and the rest of nature. It is this rift that must be healed, through conscious social planning of our economic activity and resources in a sustainable way with the biosphere. This means overthrowing capital and the capitalist class.

Another recent example of the way capitalism exacerbates problems was the outbreak of the Covid pandemic. The industrial production of food in unsanitary conditions may have led to the emergence of COVID in China. Globalisation – particularly the massive increase in long haul air flights for both cargo and people – means a much more rapid spread of viruses. Austerity means that health services are in poor shape to respond to additional pressures. Pressure to continue engaging and competing in a globalised capitalist economy creates incentives for governments to lie about emerging diseases. We saw some governments, particularly in the Global South, respond to Covid by imposing repression, not to defend the health of the population, but to protect themselves from desperate hungry people in societies where the informal economy is the main means of survival for the majority of people. Separately, anti-science propaganda is a key tool for the radical right to pitch themselves as an anti-establishment force. They used their anti-science platform to mobilise large numbers in several countries around anti-vax views – while spreading more general conspiracy theories too.

In addition to exacerbating the socio-economic origins and consequences of pandemics, capitalism also determines the health implications of disease in accordance with its exploitative value system. Black people and/or women are usually the great majority of both essential workers and service users – as such Covid deepened existing inequalities. Those living in overcrowded accommodation, using public transport or working on the Covid front lines were more likely to be subject to (re-)infection, women's disproportionate role in social reproduction was reinforced in households with children when schools were closed. Pandemics are an inevitable consequence of the environmental crisis, so we can expect that Covid is not the last – and not necessarily the worst – we will face in the years ahead.

What is often overlooked when discussing the consequences of the environmental crisis are the people at society's margins. During the Covid pandemic, eugenics-based policies were adopted that saw older and disabled people deemed expendable. Emergency planning failed to be inclusive, promoting the 'survival of the fittest'.

Despite the daily terrifying news of climate and environmental crisis we refuse to collapse into despair or despondency. We also reject the view that humanity and the planet is doomed – humans are capable of wonderful acts that can change the world but as long as we exist under capitalism we are turned against ourselves and our own environment.

How has capitalism responded to this crisis?

Because the environmental crisis is integral to capitalism, those in charge cannot envisage an alternative. All their plans and proposals have failed to tackle global warming. The Conference of Parties, launched in 1995 to prevent runaway global warming and other environmental crises, has proven unable to prevent the domination of capital from continuing its destruction. More carbon has been released into the atmosphere since the Kyoto Protocols in 1997 than in the previous two hundred years of industrial capitalism. COP 26 pledged to fight deforestation in 2021, then deforestation accelerated the year after. COP28 in Bahrain was headed by Sultan Ahmed Al Jaber, the boss of UAE oil giant ADNOC – institutional capture at its finest.

The capitalist response to the environmental crisis is not just ineffective; it is part of the problem because it is wrapped in the logic of their system. Because bosses believe 'the market' is what works, they implement cap and trade and other forms of carbon trading where companies pollute less can then sell their excess rights to pollute to others. For the first years of its existence Tesla made no profit on its cars – it made money selling pollution credits to other car companies. Or take the example of the EU's Climate Exchange, a futures market buying and selling carbon emissions – only capitalism could create a financial market for pollution! These cap and trade schemes have made some people a lot of money and singularly failed to prevent increases in greenhouse gas emissions. Capitalism is the kind of economic system where when the icecaps melt, the first thing carbon companies do is send exploration vessels to survey for previously untapped oil and gas reserves. Capitalism is a system where someone will sell you a life jacket as the water levels rise and flood you out of your home.

Green washing is the compliment vice pays to virtue. Companies that know their economic activity harms the environment, invest millions in corporate propaganda to promote the idea that they care about the environment. When it comes to profits and market share, corporations lie outright, and cover up their impact. Exxon knew about global warming in 1977, a decade before it became a public issue. Volkswagen lied about the emissions of its 'clean diesel' cars. Coca Cola launched a 'green' drink (Coca Cola Life) and promotes itself as sustainable when it is one of the biggest plastic polluters on the planet. If corporations were people, they would be guiltless psychopaths, selfishly pursuing their agenda without thought to the 'externalities' of their activities.

Corporations' failure to live up to their claims is not always just the personal failure of liars and hypocrites seeking to get rich. With the best will in the world, companies cannot completely pivot towards renewables because the way our world is currently structured is an insurmountable barrier to those changes. Companies have to make profits to survive, the money flows where the returns on investment are best. COP can meet and pass new protocols or treaties but the division of the world into discrete and competing nation states undermines each and every pledge made.

Green capitalism is a dangerous illusion. Super profits for petrochemical giants are not seriously challenged by governments. It is technically illegal in most countries to nationalise profitable companies without paying massive compensation to shareholders. Even the attempts to establish a 'green capital' that directs investment into emerging markets like renewable energies face structural obstacles. Corporations have a fiduciary duty to shareholders which actively prevent investments in anything that doesn't guarantee a certain rate of profit, these are called 'hurdle rates'. Emerging markets like green energy are often downgraded by credit rating agencies, making investment harder to guarantee. But even if these obstacles could be overcome, it would just make green energy another area for massive speculation and financial gambling. Governments have been forced to mitigate every financial danger that any new infrastructure might face. This has often led to soaring public costs for everything from new power stations to railway networks, as the private sector gets all the reward and none of the responsibility for late running or project overspends. Emerging "growth" market logic fails to shift energy production globally. Investors prioritise diversification of portfolios to guarantee return on investments instead of a serious organised transition towards renewables. Shell abandoned its Research and Development into renewables for the simple reason it could not guarantee return on investment to ensure value for shareholders. By the ruthless logic of capitalism, profit comes first no matter the cost.

Green capitalism relies heavily on new technology to be implemented to offset the damage. We reject approaches that *rely* on techno-fixes. As long as technology is in the hands of corporations or billionaires it will not create a better world. New innovations like biofuels were meant to replace carbon but require huge deforestation to make land available for agriculture and do not necessarily reduce fossil fuel production, even if they do sometimes reduce CO2 emissions. Heads of oil companies aggressively promote carbon capture and storage (CCS) because it will allow them to keep freely polluting whilst other capitalists who run the CCS sector make money sucking their greenhouse gases out of the air. But the CCS sector is sold on a false promise, as there is no way existing CCS technologies can capture the amount of fossil fuels currently being emitted at a fast enough rate to prevent catastrophic climate change. If the oil company owned by the president of COP28 ran at full capacity between 2023-2030 it would take over 340 years to remove the CO_2 it produced using carbon capture.

Green capitalism replicates forms of colonialism, imagining a world where those in the global north live with the benefits of a so-called green transition in the form of clean cities with electric cars and renewable energy. But simply replacing fuel-powered with electric vehicles, without a substantial reduction in the number of vehicles on the road, is not the answer. The production of electric vehicles places other demands on the environment, metals such as lithium and cobalt are required to make EV batteries, an electric vehicle also requires four times as much copper as a fuel-powered vehicle of the same size. If left unchecked, the environmental devastation caused by the development of new extractivist projects to supply 'green' metals for electric vehicles will fall disproportionally on those in the global south. Cobalt, lithium and copper are sourced primarily from poorer countries – and certainly sourced at the highest profit due to the exploitative working conditions prevalent in those regions.

However, there is resistance. Fears of environmental destruction caused mass opposition and protests in Panama against the Canadian owned Cobre Panamá copper mine which recently forced the country's Supreme Court to shut down the mine. In Ecuador and the Democratic Republic of Congo, unregulated mining has destroyed indigenous communities as gangster capitalists force people from the land to start extraction. Also, green capitalism does not confront the military industrial complex or the reality of imperialism as a global system of exploitation and plunder.

Given the way environmentally destructive capitalism seems inescapable, we have no hesitation labelling capitalism a death cult. This is not hyperbole. The point of a cult is that you think it is the sole truth and cannot understand anything outside of it. The cult leaders tell you that there is no alternative, no other way to live. Give everything to the cult. This means whilst capitalism is an economic system that is degrading and destroying the basis of life on the one planet we can live on, the people in charge can only implement changes that make sense *within* the logic of the system. The capitalist class cannot escape the logic of their system and they hold all the power, giving the impression that there is no way out of this mess. This is why the efforts to stop global warming and environmental devastation have so far been failures.

Capitalism relies on scarcity

The problem under capitalism is one of "managed" scarcity by the ruling class. Investment and production fulfil the needs of the system for continued economic growth and profitability, rather than the needs of the majority of the population. Billions of us live precarious lives; existing pay-cheque to pay-cheque if we can "contribute our ability to labour" in the capitalist economic system, or live in outright poverty dependent upon state social services to survive (where they exist). Some of us have comfortable lives, but all that can change with the vagaries of market economics, you can lose your job, inflation can impede access to energy, heating and food, your mortgage payments skyrocket, you get into debt – the threat of scarcity, of having less – hangs over us.

On our planet, there is natural scarcity and capitalist-manufactured scarcity. Natural scarcity involves hard to produce resources or those that are in limited supply (fresh water, oil, coal, helium, copper, lithium). No matter what economic system, we only have certain reserves left to extract. The other kind of scarcity is a product of our current economic system, such as wages or housing. Whilst the capitalist class enjoys a life of untrammelled luxury where money is no object, the rest of us worry about the end of the month. Around one third of workers in Britain have no savings – wages and benefits are both too low to allow people to save. Time is also scarce, many of us work long hours to make ends meet, leaving little time to enjoy our lives. Scarcity is why people buy cheap Ikea furniture which doesn't last, whilst the company systematically engages in deforestation. The false economy of fast fashion is one of the most polluting industries on the planet. This isn't to condemn people's consumption habits; this is the reality of our economic society. Rather than moral criticism, we need an alternative way to live.

Because capitalism constructs and defines scarcity, it structures our thinking- how we see the world. It is the basis of reactionary thinking, that we only have a certain amount so we have to jealously guard it. Hatred of migrants or refugees or people on social security are all defined by anger about people 'taking' things. Taking jobs, wages or housing, taking money they don't deserve from the collective pot because they haven't been a productive worker. Scarcity informs our understanding of relative privilege. It is when a white male worker who has little in the grand scheme of things jealously guards what he has from others, when a British person sees themselves as superior to someone from a poorer country, even if they are themselves relatively poor. Some industrial and extractivist workers reject climate advocacy because they see it as a threat to their jobs.

This is the background to the backlash against the growing movement to resist ecocide. Angry motorists attacking climate activists, people sharing conspiracy theories against climate scientists, people hating Greta Thunberg, even trade unions advocating a 'jobs first' policy – all come from a fear of change and a fear that the 'climate agenda' will take things away from people. This is why right wing populists label environmental politics 'middle class'; it is a luxury to care about biodiversity when real people struggle to survive on meagre wages. We say it is the same fight, that the people polluting the oceans and soil and sky are the same class that won't pay a decent wage. Why do these rich media owners and their politicians devote so much time to making you hate refugees, and promoting the kind of arguments that benefit the super-rich shareholders of petrochemical giants?

These dynamics are driving the growth of the far right internationally. Faced with social decline as capitalism fails to meet our basic needs, centre left and liberal governments have repeatedly failed to rise to the challenge because they are locked into the logic of the system, advocating globalisation and failing to deliver on promised social changes. This creates spaces for reactionary populist and far right forces to emerge to 'save the nation', a new generation of leaders from 'outside the establishment' threaten the status quo (from the right); Trump, Bolsonaro, Modi, Milei and Meloni. Waiting in the wings are people like Le Pen in France. All of them are climate change deniers or delayers to some degree. They know that to really confront the climate is to confront capital as an economic force and they are defenders of capitalism, this leads them to wage a war on what the they call 'woke' climate science. They point to higher household bills and blame climate policies. They direct hate at migrants to deflect attention from the ones who have real power.

This is why a key aim of an ecosocialist future is to abolish manufactured scarcity and in doing so to abolish the social divisions that it causes and to create a world of radical abundance where the entire waged, commodified economy is replaced by a society where we produce what everyone wants and needs.

Why Ecosocialism?

Humans deserve a good quality of life, and we must preserve our environment for future generations. This means ensuring a sustainable relationship with the natural world, including other life forms. We cannot prevent further rises in global warming or provide a just existence for humanity so long as capitalism continues. This is why we define our project as one of ecosocialism.

We use ecosocialism because the ecocide threatened by the capitalist system is the defining character of our epoch and as such we need to clearly orientate the socialist project to the struggle for our future survival. It also marks a clear differentiation from the old productivist forms of some left wing movements where industrial capacity was prioritised without proper consideration of planetary limits. For us, ecosocialism is based on democratic decision making by the majority – producers and consumers. Unlike the one party Stalinist states of the 20th century, ecosocialist societies will have free association of people to argue for specific and particular interests, with their views incorporated into democratic social planning. We are much more cautious of the way that some previous generations believed modern technology would enable us to manipulate the environment to our will with no consequences. This has been called Prometheanism, the supremacy of technology over nature in a way that ignores ecology.

But we also reject primitivist proposals. We cannot build a sustainable future for humanity through a 'retreat to nature' or requiring everyone to become subsistence farmers. A world of only rural subsistence farming is static. We aim to restore the balance between town and country, rural and metropolitan, urban and farm.

Ecosocialism is a society where the economy has been taken out of the hands of the capitalist class through being socialised, becoming a collectively owned part of human society. It is a world where we have participatory democracy over economic decisions and where we are progressively dismantling the racist and sexist social division of labour under capitalism. Any ecosocialist planned economy will have to grapple with competing demands and challenges that will require us to make informed decisions at every level, from local to global. The debates over investment or production, over meat, over what kind of energy we use, will require an open and informed discussion, not top down diktat by unelected bureaucrats. The end goal of this is to create a fair economy that is consistent with human needs within a sustainable relationship to other life forms and the environment.

Any serious project to address the degradation of the environment caused by capital must prioritise mitigating the impact of climate change on the global south, and achieve the goal of ending the unequal relationship between imperialist metropoles and neo-colonies. It means a clear and unequivocal support for the struggles of working people across the world, especially in the poorer areas of the global south – mostly populated by people of colour – against capitalism, and how its destruction of their environment will impact on them.

Mass migratory patterns caused by climate change will be a significant feature of politics in the next decades and the fight against fascism and far right politics, as well as the need to tear down national borders and build global solidarity, will be decisive.

Ecosocialism must include eco-feminist perspectives because the impact of environmental degradation will be exacerbated by class and gender oppression. As we fight for a new world we must build movements of solidarity with women who make up the majority of the unwaged working class whilst others suffer the double burden of waged labour and household work. Millions of working women globally do work that capital considers unproductive and difficult to commoditise (e.g. reproduction, care, subsistence). Bringing those women into waged work is a reform within the current system, but a revolutionary approach is to fight to build a different economy based on decommodified labour, focusing on necessary work as part of a social plan.

To be against productivist 'socialism' means to challenge the idea that we take the economic production and distribution that capitalism has created and simply 'run it under workers' control'. The massively productive capacities of capital (all the factories, workshops, tools, supply chain, complex planning arrangements, etc) are geared towards only one thing – profit. It will not be sustainable to simply lay hold of the readymade economic machinery and use it for socialism.

Ecosocialism replaces profit with measurable social and environmental needs, for instance human happiness and aligning human society within planetary boundaries again. We start from what is sustainable and necessary for a good life for every human on the planet. This means guarantees on quality of life for every single human – and we build a global economy that can sustain that. For instance we could aim for a global energy usage of 3.5 kilowatt/ person, powered by renewables and geothermal. We note that global energy consumption was 25,343 terawatts in 2021, and the sun continuously provides 173,000 terawatts of solar energy. Harnessing this will be central to stopping runaway global warming.

The ecosocialist vision of a future human society rejects the pursuit of economic growth as an end in itself. This contains elements of a degrowth argument, though we are not specifically setting out the goal of 'degrowing' the economy. As Michael Lowy has argued "degrowth in itself is not an alternative economic and social perspective: it does not define what kind of society will replace the present system. Some proponents of degrowth would ignore the issue of capitalism, focusing only on productivism and consumerism, defining the culprit as 'The West,' 'Enlightenment,' or 'Prometheanism'."

This is a crucial difference between capitalism and socialism. There will need to be massive investment in renewables, transport and housing to rebalance the world economy in a sustainable way and improve lives for billions around the planet. But investment under capitalism is driven by profitability, or otherwise it has to be guaranteed with significant (often reluctant) government backing. We propose to socialise the economy to allow for democratic and rational decision making over investments to improve our communities.

We will need to restructure the economy as part of the ecosocialist strategy. We advocate a planned reduction of destructive and less necessary forms of production and consumption by rich economies (such as fossil fuels, fast fashion and advertising). This would reduce the energy and materials used, allowing for a rapid transition to low-carbon economies at a rate quick enough to stop ecological breakdown, redistributing income and resources fairly to global populations.

This is a positive program of an ecosocialist society, based on democratic planning, self-management, production of use values instead of commodities, gratuity of basic services, and free time for the development of human desires and capacities. It is a society without exploitation, class domination, patriarchy, and all forms of social exclusion. It is a society without exploitation, class, systemic misogyny and sexism, racism, disablism and LGBTQIA+ phobia

We support Green New Deal demands that are achievable reforms to help offset the worst excesses of capitalism. But we do not believe there is a route to socialism through New Deal policies. Too many Green New Deals are simply pitched at the level of government policy – as socialists we want to build movements around the demands, mobilising workers and popular forces to fight for their implementation and to go beyond the logic of capitalism. We also oppose Green New Deals that replicate the legacy of colonial extraction, strip mining parts of the global south to build green tech for the richer nations. We need a genuine global solution based on democratic planning of production and resources to manage these issues.

We support the decommodification and democratisation of our economy. *Democratising* the economy and the relationship to labour requires a new vision of work; beyond waged labour, it encompasses all kinds of labour and a fight for our self-actualisation as human beings, with full control of our social lives. We fight for the decommodification of energy, transport education, food, healthcare and housing.

There is mounting evidence that we have already crossed various tipping points to prevent runaway ecological decline. It is no surprise that some of the richest men in the word are obsessed with space travel – they can see what their economic system is causing. If we are on a runaway train, it makes the case for ecosocialism stronger. We cannot continue to live in a planet dominated by the chaos and inequality of capitalism as devastating weather impacts our societies. We will need conscious planning, democratic decision making and collective organisation to survive as a species, as has always been the case, to ensure what resources we have left are distributed fairly and we can ensure the survival of as many species as we can. None of this can be left to enlightened entrepreneurs to 'fix things' for a profit.

Why the working class?

It is popular to claim the working class is either no longer with us or only exists in small towns and is exclusively made up of racists who hate foreigners. This is intended to confuse people about what is really going on and to frustrate attempts to build movements against capitalism.

As ecosocialists the working class is crucial to any revolutionary change. The working class is not just factory workers; it is made up of those of us who rely on wages to live, who own few or no assets, those that carry out unpaid essential work in the home and in care, those that are exploited for money by others. The working class is the largest group of people on the planet with the greatest social weight. Industry, commerce, healthcare, transport, local amenities, nothing could function without working people. Because we need to restructure the global economy, we start from those that work in that economy as the main agents of change.

The working class is not a blood type or only defined by culture - football or opera? It is about how you are forced to exist by those in power and how you struggle against them. Many people who consider themselves middle class in professions like teaching or doctors are forced into trade unions to defend their living conditions, just as much as people in precarious employment. Capitalism promises social mobility, but increasingly those once prosperous middle class jobs are becoming 'proletarianised', amongst the biggest strikes in Britain in 2023 were those by barristers and doctors.

Capitalism repeatedly exposes itself not as a system that provides for all, but as one based on exploitation and oppression, one not only with class differences but class antagonisms. Capitalism forces workers to unite to fight for their class interests, from wages to healthcare to a shorter working week, workers know their strength is in their collective power. This is why workers form trade unions and cooperatives, establish political parties and campaigns to advocate and struggle for what they need.

The working class is crucial to an ecosocialist strategy because we want to totally transform the economic relations of production, distribution and exchange. This means conscious mass action by the working class in all its myriad forms. We mean the broadest category of working class, not as merely blue collar (white, male) industrial workers, but a universal category, every human being that needs to sell their labour power, that is reduced to the status of a commodity by capital, that works informally with unpaid care and social work – all will benefit from a new world where labour power is not commodified.

We support workers taking action over their economic conditions, wages, living standards, and any social movement or campaign that emerges to improve people's lives, for instance housing or their local environment. We fight to link the struggles up, and to politicise 'industrial' disputes, to transform struggles into a broader political fight against capitalism.

While they are not always part of the working class exploited by capital, we also support the struggle of indigenous peoples against thefts of their territories by fossil fuel developers, mineral extractors, and giant agribusinesses. These assaults and displacements not only lead to ecocide, but also to the destruction of large areas of the vital natural world, and its animal inhabitants and the reduction of indigenous peoples to penury/impoverishment.

The movement we need to win

Any mass ecosocialist movement must do two things. First, fight for changes in the here and now that slow the destruction of the biosphere by capital, giving us more time to organise and coordinate. Secondly, promote forms of organisation that target capital directly.

We favour a mass movement coordinated internationally that struggles for immediate reforms but also looks to a different kind of world. We want a fighting unity of all 'single issue' environmental campaigns and their integration into a working class movement that is organised around not just industrial demands but also political ones.

We fight for a movement to tackle the big issues; expropriation of business and private wealth, socialising housing and land, ending the market economy, dismantling imperialism, fighting for abolition of borders, militarism and authoritarian policing practices, and social transformation of the economy from the ground up.

Whilst socialists must engage in the mass organisations of the working class such as trade unions, we recognise that institutions like the Labour Party in Britain and trade unions are integrated into capitalism. They seek to reform it but often it is capitalism that 'reforms' them, turning them into neutered organisations obedient to capital.

Capital can only rule over us because it divides us along gender, ethnicity, nationality or any other pretext. These aren't artificial divisions, in the real world there are real wage gaps and opportunity gaps for different workers that bind better off workers to capitalism whilst excluding and dismissing others.

Trade unions need to become leaders of wider struggles, not just focus on the terms and conditions of their members in narrow 'trade disputes'. Trade unions should align and bring their resources into social movements, around housing, abortion rights and against pollution. When it comes to wage struggles the unions must move beyond sectional disputes and focus on fighting for decent wages for *all* workers, on improving living standards and for a universal conception of what it means to be human. Only in this way can we transform narrow trade union struggles into political struggles that create a real workers' movement, not just a trade union movement.

Democracy and self-organisation

We oppose any restrictions on democratic rights or workers' rights to organise and express themselves. We are in favour of workers using their power to force progressive change – for instance, the Green Ban movement in Australia where workers took action on climate issues. The experience of the Lucas Plan in the 1970s when aerospace workers threatened with redundancy developed their own green transition plan is an inspiration for us. More recently the GKN factory in Florence has been hugely popular internationally as workers managed their own eco-transition from bottom up. This means politicising strikes and arguing for workers to take over bankrupt or failing industries under their direct control.

Likewise we are opposed to restrictions on the right to protest more generally.

We actively support the autonomous self-organisation of socially oppressed groups; women, Black people, disabled people, young people and others must be able to organise and advocate for demands relevant to specific oppressions.

We recognise that the UK is made of different nations and the environmental struggles will take their own forms. There will be specific demands in the nations as well as international action – none of the problems that global warming raises can be solved nationally.

A new kind of political power

We must win political power. Social movements are crucially for slowing down environmental degradation and cultivating counter-power but on their own they cannot achieve what we need.

We back any reforms where they create meaningful, positive change, but we reject the idea that the capitalist state can simply be repurposed for socialist transformation. The modern state as it exists is there to maintain the existing property relations and capital accumulation of the powers that be.

Whilst promoting ecosocialist policies in Parliament is useful, the capitalist state (in our case Parliament or the devolved legislatures) as it exists is incapable of implementing the transformative anticapitalist plan required. Its civil servants, security apparatus, judges, and courts are wedded to our existing system. It is tied by a million cords to capitalism and protecting an economy based on capital accumulation. The legal and political framework of capitalism — based on the sanctity of private property — is totally at odds with the world we need to build to have a sustainable future, based on commons and common ownership alongside universal services.

This means we need a new kind political power, based on a mass popular participatory democracy that we are fighting for in the existing social movements and workers' struggles. We challenge the 'sovereignty' of Parliament and seek to replace it with more direct democracy in workplaces and communities. We have seen the danger of becoming managers of a capitalist state through parliaments in the fate of Syriza in Greece or the Greens in Germany – despite the best intentions. These parties ended up becoming exactly what they opposed under the pressure of capitalism and austerity.

We need popular democratic forums that can form a new political basis for decision making. This is not toothless citizens' assemblies, but forums committed to a new kind of power. It means decision making that isn't in the hands of MPs or local councillors who are, in reality, big business and the corporate elites, but is rooted in our communities and workplaces. But such forums need genuine political power, this is why we need to socialise property and take over businesses and banks. We also need mass educational programmes regarding ecological sustainability to combat climate denialists and to enable us to effectively manage economic decision making.

A sustainable relationship with the environment

An ecosocialist manifesto should prioritise the vision of a future world where we are free from commodification and alienation and can live in a sustainable relationship to the planet. This means not just talking about the tools we will use (socialising the economy, democratic planning) but why we use them and what kind of world we want to build with them.

Labour processes: Instead of labour being directed only towards accumulating profit – regardless of the environmental consequences – the allocation of labour time for social projects, whether building train tracks or fishing, will be directed by clearer estimations of human wants. For example, a particular area needs 100 km of railroads and 2,000 tonnes of fish as determined by local decision mechanisms. This reduces wasteful overproduction. When we organise the economy beyond the drive for profit, we can better understand the effects of economic processes on our world. The potential carbon cost is included in the work because the work is socially directed. There are no externalities.

Spatial: the division between town and country, or urban and rural, is incredibly damaging for the environment. This is not to say that the countryside is some idyllic paradise, and urban centres are bad, it is to say that the relationship between them is antagonistic and destructive. A socialist plan for the countryside would see farming collectively run without the need for dangerous agricultural methods caused by profit-seeking. Cities would be reorganised to be less wasteful, for instance, housing would only be built for need after all the available housing had been allocated.

Temporal: People won't have to rush around to get to places because of ridiculous work commitments demanded by capital. Life can be more relaxed because leisure time will be the majority of our time. This will allow travel to be at once more luxurious and more environmentally-friendly: trains to be used instead of planes, and air conditioned coaches instead of cars.

To challenge these dynamics within capitalism is to challenge the entire logic of capital to always deepen, accelerate and accumulate.

The main task is socialisation of the economy. This means that there is democratic control over the social surplus and the balance between immediate needs (consumption) and future needs (investment). We can then shift the economy from production of exchange values as commodities for profit to a society where we make things based on democratically decided human need. This will massively reduce economic throughput and output, helping realign human activity to a more sustainable relationship with the environment.

Social control allows us to implement a just transition from polluting extractivist work through retraining workers and retooling industry. Ending the profit motive will allow us to stop planned obsolescence, the principle of 'renew, rebuilt, fix and recycle' for all relevant consumable goods. We will end unnecessary waste and unproductive labour to focus on a society built around public goods and use values.

Socialisation means all externalities can be integrated into decision making over production and distribution allowing us to calculate the proper cost of any economic activity.

Alongside this we need complete socialisation of the land – an end to private ownership of land. Currently just 25,000 landowners – around 0.04% of the population – own half of the land in England. Socialisation of the land would massively reduce house values, lowering rent considerably. Any loss of value for homeowners would be dealt with through nationalisation of banks and restructuring their mortgages.

A rational, social economy means decommodifying things we need. Food and other essentials that we can produce in abundance we can proceed to make freely available through socialising production and providing good wages to producers.

The fight for universal basic services

The idea of Universal Basic Income (UBI) has become popular in recent years but we do not see it as a plausible route to ecosocialism. Essentially, UBI leaves production of goods and services under control of the market, that is the private sector, and hence profitability criteria remain intact. So UBI would not allow us to achieve the level of production of goods and services and that means there is no guarantee we alter what and how much is produced to fulfil the our needs. Moreover, whilst we fight for higher wages and better social security for everyone, UBI only redistributes revenue, not power. To achieve the redistribution of revenue would require such a seismic shift in class relations it would open up the possibility of a revolution – so why stop at just getting extra money?

Instead, we support a fight for Universal Basic Services (UBS) as a demand that points to the transition to ecosocialism even under capitalism. Universal Basic Services are necessary to sustain and enable each citizen's material safety, opportunity to contribute, or participate in the decision-making processes. The UBS model extends the notion of a social safety net to include those elements necessary to fulfil a larger social role. We want to eliminate disability, a part and parcel of the capitalist economic system that requires those without wealth to sell their ability to labour as their “contribution” to the capitalist economic system. Throughout their lives, people will always need access to social support and assistance. While we support the idea of UBS, we must also recognise that people have different needs for services throughout their lives. Disabled people and older people will always have greater needs for social support and assistance and "basic services" will be insufficient. We endorse the right to services free at the point of demand, as in capitalism, for whatever services are needed to include all members of society; the production and development of services to be democratically determined by service users and providers in a co-productive manner by local communities and funded nationally.

The NHS is an existing example of the right to healthcare, though under capitalism the principle of universal healthcare is always being eroded and undermined. A fundamental shift must be the development of co-produced community-based sustainable services. Such services would replace the oppressive ageist and disablist, so-called Social Care System. It would also add libraries, parks and art galleries and museums as part of the development of inclusive living. As such, we must discuss social support and assistance, and education, including childcare and libraries. We do not want a focus just on individual consumption, it has to be about collective production and the use of resources under democratic control to produce the goods and services for the benefit of everyone.

Universal Basic Services are not predicated on your ability to pay, and we utterly reject the concept of means testing. The poor should access the same high quality services as the rich, the difference is the rich pay more through taxation to fund these services. Means testing is humiliating for the poor ('prove to us how poor you are') and cuts against universal access to things we consider good for everyone.

The IPCC has already identified the importance of a shift in economic thinking towards UBS, that "development targeted to basic needs and well-being for all entails less carbon-intensity than GDP-focused growth". Economies of scale around universal services allow for more rational economic activity in providing for human needs within planetary limits.

Free and accessible public transport

Transport is not just about getting around. Being able to move, stay connected, and access different parts of the world is a fundamental part of our humanity and we reject its commodification for profit. Under capitalism it is often expensive, frustrating and divisive. Cities are built around cars to ensure profit for car companies, and greenhouse gas emissions from cars and taxis are seven times higher than from buses. Transport is often exclusionary, too expensive for poor people and inadequately designed or provided for people with accessibility needs.

As part of a radical redesign of cities to make them more ecologically sound we need free and accessible public transport. Fewer cars, replaced by hybrid or electric buses, trains and improved cycle options will improve the quality of life in our urban areas.

All transport options need to be accessible. We cannot assume that everyone can cycle or walk. All decisions on local transport planning need to involve co-production, to meet the needs of everyone in the community.

But it isn't just cities. Better train and bus connections are crucial for overcoming the division between town and country. Providing a decent rural accessible public transport system will be revolutionary for thousands of communities and provide jobs for many.

We must reduce air travel, except for necessary long haul flights, and instead work with other countries to build high speed rail services, as well as providing people more annual leave to complete trips.

We are in favour of local democracy over our communities, but local councils have sometimes faced opposition from residents over low traffic neighbourhoods (LTNS) and other 'green measures'. This is because green measures are often seen as a 'loss', people losing options or travel rights. Local councils often don't have the money or planning powers to resolve all these concerns. This is why we need a national plan to ensure the greatest carbon neutral options for people to travel.

Farming and food

We need an end to the mass-industrialised meat, dairy and fishing agri-businesses. These three sectors are massive contributors to the climate crisis, huge consumers – and contaminators – of freshwater supplies, and the major factor driving the ecological crisis and the Sixth Great Extinction. These capitalist mega-industries have already played a huge role in creating an increasingly deadly 'metabolic rift' between humans and the rest of the natural world – of which we are a part, and on which we depend.

In particular, these mega-industries pose serious threats to biodiversity – and human health – by their ongoing destruction of natural habitats, especially of the world's remaining rainforests.

The amount of land needed to meet current levels of meat and dairy consumption is already ecologically-unsustainable. Though small -scale indigenous, peasant and regenerative animal-farming does not have such a negative impact on the natural world, such farming methods scaled-up would take even more land away from nature, but would fail to provide current levels of meat and dairy production. Thus there needs to be a massive global shift away from the level of meat and dairy consumption that exists today.

Such a shift would require far less land and far less use of freshwater. There would also be a massive reduction in animal slurry waste; the biggest single cause of freshwater pollution.

Thus a shift to a mainly plant-based diet will not only conserve what is left of the natural world but allow for a huge restoration of natural habitats and ecosystems that have already been destroyed by the large capitalist agri-businesses. Such a programme of regeneration would not only reduce the risk of further zoonotic viruses crossing over from the natural world to humans but would also create a large number of useful green jobs across the globe.

For those who value meat above all else, we will prioritise developing high standard meat substitutes, including lab grown meat.

A more secure world

Because capitalism is an unequal society that creates conditions of scarcity and alienation, people live in fear of not only poverty but also crime. People live in fear of being assaulted, robbed or even murdered.

The right wing response is to throw money at more police and prisons, locking up human beings for years on end or bringing back the death penalty. We do not accept that there are people 'born bad' or that a lifetime in prison or death sentences are the best way to deal with crime. Whilst we must take steps to ensure violent individuals do not hurt other people, the only future where we can guarantee human happiness is to understand why people are violent or why there is anti-social behaviour. This will involve combatting poverty and wider mental health research and social provision.

Years of austerity have ravaged our communities, with more money sent on late intervention for young people than on preventative measures. The government spent £25.3bn on the police service in 2023 whilst local government budgets for social care, youth services, local amenities are close to collapse.

But police do not really solve most crimes yet are increasingly militarised, they're there to defend an unequal society, not solve the problems that lead to crime. Recent governments have empowered the police with even greater means to prevent demonstrations, arrest protestors and muzzle opposition. The right wing obsesses about cancel culture on social media whilst cheering authoritarian governments who are strengthening the power of the police and prisons.

Similarly, prisons do not rehabilitate and can brutalise people into greater levels of social alienation and violence. The law and order agenda is a front for regressive, usually racist, policies that flood the streets with armed police and build massive prison complexes rather than deal with the underlying social problems.

When we call for a more secure world, that does not mean more institutions like the police. It means ending precariousness and poverty, providing mental health services and pastoral care. It means no more fear and anxiety due to scarcity and alienated individualism. An ecosocialist approach focuses on shifting resources towards community cohesion, improving the quality of our lives, raising wages and access to more public services, amazing cultural events and institutions alongside parks and leisure. Dealing with crime prevention firstly through a public health approach is not only more effective but saves valuable resources as well as offering people more chances for social rehabilitation. It makes life safer for everyone. What measures for security are required should be democratically organised and based on principles of social justice not harsh authoritarianism.

Internationalism

Although this manifesto focuses on the struggle in England and Cymru/Wales, it is clear that this is an international fight, a global battle for the future. Given the scale of the crisis, internationalism is not just a dream of the left; it is a serious matter for practical action.

We believe in uniting workers across borders, building a genuine global movement to overthrow the dictatorship of capital in every country. We oppose and reject divisions of the working class by nationality, religion, skin colour or anything else. The bosses exploit these divisions to turn us against each other, helped by their allies on the far right.

We are in solidarity with migrants and refugees fleeing poverty, war and climate breakdown. The cutting edge of the far right in the present climate is to blame the poor from other countries for 'taking our jobs' or running down public services. In reality it is the capitalist class and their politicians that do this, exploiting workers and imposing austerity whilst they fly on their private jets to holiday on their own islands.

As part of our international obligations as an ecosocialist society we will prioritise aid and funding for political and civil society organisations that are fighting for similar principles of ecosocialist change.

We will cancel all debts owed by third world governments. If any debt is owed it is by the capitalists in the imperialist states to the global south, for centuries they have profited from colonial and imperialist plunder and super-exploitation and continue to do so. We fully support demands from the global south for imperialist reparations, whether it refers to climate, slavery, or other reparation demands.

As we globally reduce reliance on fossil fuels the richer nations will have to work with those countries who based their economies so heavily on extractivism of fossil fuels. Countries like Nigeria, Venezuela, Ecuador and Iraq will need to restructure their economies around radically different priorities and there needs to be a global effort to ensure these climate transitions are fair.

To fight for this we need international organisation and coordination. We pledge to work to establish a global ecosocialist international and provide considerable resources towards it. We want to help unite revolutionary ecosocialist forces globally as part of a strategy to combat international capitalism.

AN EMERGENCY PLAN

We are in a climate emergency, as serious as any war. And just as the British government took extraordinary measures during World War Two, an ecosocialist government will take emergency means now to resist global warming and environmental degradation to the point of social collapse.

The goals of an emergency plan are to reduce carbon emissions, mitigate the ecological crisis, and protect communities from the negative impact of global warming and environmental degradation. This requires a twin-track approach. The first is to ensure emergency planning is in place to protect communities from flooding, intense heat, starvation, pandemics, etc. These plans must be transparent, co-produced with communities, and ensure no one is left behind. The second track focuses on preventing the deepening of the crisis, for instance ending all new oil and gas licences and cancelling existing ones. These necessary acts are only possible when large parts of the economy have been socialised, removed from the private sector and begun to be organised under a plan for society based on participatory democracy. However, we can still fight for them even under a capitalist society, as we point the way to a better world.

Some examples of ecosocialist demands include:

- An end to new oil and gas licenses. Keep the carbon in the ground! End all government subsidies to highly polluting industries. A green transition for workers in extractivist and highly polluting industries towards other forms of work, with comprehensive and free retraining and education or fully paid early retirement made available.

- A planned and rapid shift from fossil fuel energy towards renewables based on wind, solar and geothermal.
- The combined carbon emissions from the global military industrial complex is one of the main driving forces in global warming. We stand for a complete reduction in the total military budget as part of a global coordinated effort to move towards a de-weaponised world.
- Expand the public sector as part of increasing Universal Basic Services.
- Significant reduction in the length of the working week with no loss of pay to soak up any unemployment and improve our quality of lives. Introduce a social plan to eventually reduce the working week further.
- Repeal all the anti union laws in the UK and replace them with a bill of rights guaranteeing workers' and trade union freedoms as well as comprehensive improvements around wages, sick pay and holiday.
- Take over all large agribusinesses and reorganise farming around more sustainable models less reliant on intensive inputs of pesticides and chemicals. We have to work actively to renew soil fertility. The key point is to take the profit motive out of farming and food supply.

- Abolish the patent system and, in particular, stop all patents for healthcare and on technologies concerning energy conversion and storage.
- Fund the retrofitting of all homes and offices with heat pumps and insulation.
- Make bus travel accessible and free and invest heavily in new bus routes especially in rural areas.
- State regulation of housing, including rent controls and massive taxes on second and third homes. Give local councils the resources and legal powers to compulsory purchase homes empty for more than a year to clear the waiting lists.
- An end to investments by finance capital in extractivist and polluting industries, no more subsidies for fossil capital.
- An end to speculation on food as a commodity.
- A ban on throwing away usable commodities like clothing just because they are 'end of line'.
- An end to food waste by supermarkets, a ban on supermarkets throwing away food.
- An end to single use plastics including plastic water bottles.
- Release all climate prisoners. Restore all rights to protest.
- Statutory paid time off for trade union green reps and environmental officers.
- Refugee status to the victims of ecological/climate disasters; full respect for the democratic rights of LL refugees including freedom of movement and settlement.

Anti*Capitalist Resistance—What we stand for

Anti*Capitalist Resistance is a revolutionary Marxist organisation in England & Cymru/Wales.

The world is facing an unprecedented and interrelated crisis of economic collapse, social decay, grotesque inequality, mass impoverishment, growing militarisation, and creeping authoritarianism. Capitalist liberal institutions and parties can no longer sustain the status quo as the drive for profit eats away at our society and deepens a metabolic rift between people and planet.

Extreme inequality is out of control. There are more billionaires than ever before. Millions live in poverty whilst the super rich go into space. Meanwhile, the world's poorest get even poorer as governments bail out private corporations and cut back on education and health. This is no accident, or just the result of greed. It is built into the logic of capitalism, a system built on profit and exploitation of people and planet.

Change is urgent. We need mass movements to win victories for democracy and social, climate and economic justice. We support the greatest amount of democracy under capitalism, abolishing the monarchy and the House of Lords and supporting Proportional Representation.

We organise for action and reforms now, but also for a total reorganisation of human society on a global level.

Ecosocialism

Anti*Capitalist Resistance defines itself as ecosocialist because the ecological crisis is so profound that it redefines the socialist project. We are engaged not just in a struggle to end capitalism and for a socialist society, but also to have a viable planet. We reject the old productivism of 20th century Stalinism and Social Democracy. Instead, we fight for a stable economy that meets human needs based on the collective democratic power of producers and consumers. Such a society will be consistent with a sustainable relationship to other life forms and the environment itself.

We challenge the growth-based and consumption-driven system of capitalism, which is also responsible for the development of pandemics such as Covid-19. This task is urgent. That's why we need mass movements today that force governments to keep the rise in global warming below 1.5°C by 2030 to prevent catastrophic and irreversible climate change.

Poverty, exploitation and oppression and war are products of the capitalist system in which a tiny minority ruling class benefits from the labour of the majority. The alternative is socialism, where the wealth created is owned in common, major assets such as industry and finance are socialised and democratic planning to meet society's needs.

However, social-democratic parties like the Labour Party no longer refer to socialism and, in practice, support the continued existence of capitalism, though with occasional minor reforms to offset the worst effects of it. Social democracy in Britain is wedded to imperialism and racist border controls.

We do not believe that the USSR or China under Mao was socialist. Workers and consumers democracy is central to any genuinely socialist society and these were utterly lacking. Socialism is not possible without the fullest possible democracy. It must guarantee freedom of expression and organisation to every range of opinion, other than those who incite violence against the oppressed or the working class.

Internationalism

Anti*Capitalist Resistance is internationalist and opposes imperialism, nationalism and militarism.

Capitalism is an international system, so the struggle for socialism must be international, uniting workers of all countries. Huge corporations, some bigger than many countries, dominate the world economy. We need to organise across borders for action and solidarity. Socialists oppose imperialism- the subjugation of weaker nations by stronger ones- and support the self-determination of oppressed nations and the struggle for national liberation.

We are against racism from the state and in any other form, against immigration controls and borders, and support the struggle for migrant rights. We fight to remove the legacy of slavery and colonialism.

Anti*Capitalist Resistance supports the right of people to challenge colonialism and all forms of apartheid and to struggle for self-determination, including for the people of Palestine. We will support a united Ireland and the right to self-determination Scotland and

Cymru/Wales, up to and including independence. We are for the right for self-determination for oppressed nationalities which includes the right to self-defence and agency to choose how to conduct this struggle. We believe in unconditional– though critical- solidarity.

Liberation for the oppressed

Capitalism divides working class people along sexual, gender, ethnic, national and other distinctions; the oppressed suffer most. The most effective way to fight back is for those who directly experience discrimination to organise and lead their own struggles. Much has been achieved but not liberation. There can be no liberation without socialism, and no socialism without liberation of the oppressed. We oppose all forms of racism and ethnic division, and the way that capital racialises human society. The racist demagogues and fascist movements that seek to divide us and whip up race hate most be opposed politically and physically if necessary. We support the fight for equality whilst recognising that under capitalism full equality is impossible in a society divided by class power.

We oppose the oppression of women and women's primary responsibility for unpaid labour in social reproduction. We believe in reproductive justice and support the bodily autonomy of women and trans people. Socialists support the fight for reproductive rights, for equal pay, against male violence, and for LGBT+ rights.

We are for the creation of an inclusive society where systems, structures, and practices do not impose unnecessary social restrictions on people who experience chronic illnesses and impairment reality.

The labour movement and socialists must champion these liberation struggles as their own, while recognising the right of the oppressed to lead these struggles and formulate their own demands. We support the self-organisation of women, Black people, disabled people and LGBTIQ people to combat all forms of discrimination, oppression and bigotry.

We take the culture war seriously as a site of conflict between socialists and reactionaries. As Marxists, we believe that cultural battles are not secondary to economic ones. We oppose the right's distortion of class that defines it as a static, often reactionary identity and reassert Marx's formulation of class as a living process of struggle necessarily involving the mass agency of workers in transforming the world and thereby themselves.

Our organisation

Anti*Capitalist Resistance is a pluralist and internationalist organisation that can learn from struggles across the world. We are democratic revolutionary socialists and oppose the top-down model of 'democratic-centralist' organisation. We encourage convergence with other revolutionary Marxist activists and organisations. Anti*Capitalist Resistance aims to be rooted in the struggles of the working class and the oppressed and is committed to debate, initiative, and self-activity. In the spirit of internationalism we are an observer organisation to the Fourth International.

Anti*Capitalist Resistance bases its politics on Marxism and its perspective of revolutionary class struggle. We have a vision of a new society, one based on human freedom, as described in the Communist Manifesto "In place of the old bourgeois society, with its classes and class antagonisms, we shall have an association, in which the free development of each is the condition for the free development of all".

Links

Our website is at **anticapitalistresistance.org**

You can join us at **anticapitalistresistance.org/join**

Follow us on **Twitter**, **Facebook** and **Instagram**

Please also visit **ecosocialism-conference.org** for campaigning work around workers and ecosocialist revolution.

A*CR is part of the Global Ecosocialist Network which you can find at **globalecosocialistnetwork.net**